# Extremely WEIRD

## MICRO MONSTERS

Text by Sarah Lovett

John Muir Publications
Santa Fe, New Mexico

**Special thanks to Gene Harrell, Biology Consultant, Santa Fe, New Mexico**

John Muir Publications, P.O. Box 613, Santa Fe, New Mexico 87504
© 1993 by John Muir Publications
All rights reserved. Published 1993
Printed in the United States of America

First edition. First printing August 1993.
                First TWG printing August 1993.
Printed on recycled paper.

Library of Congress Cataloging-in-Publication Data
Lovett, Sarah, 1953-
    Extremely weird micro monsters / Sarah Lovett.
       p.   cm.
    Includes index.
    Summary: Photographs and illustrations
introduce twenty unusual microscopic organisms,
including the red blood cell, influenza virus, head
louse, and red spider mite.
    ISBN 1-56261-120-8 : $9.95
    1. Microbiology—Juvenile literature.
    2. Microscopy—Juvenile literature.
    [1. Microorganisms.  2. Microbiology.]  I. Title.
    QR57.L685 1993
    576—dc20            93-19591
                        CIP
                        AC

Illustrations: Mary Sundstrom, Beth Evans
Extremely Weird Logo Art: Peter Aschwanden
Design: Sally Blakemore
Typography: Ken Wilson
Printer: Guynes Printing Company

Distributed to the book trade by
W. W. Norton & Co., Inc.
500 Fifth Avenue
New York, New York 10110

Distributed to the education market by
The Wright Group
19201 120th Avenue N.E.
Bothell, Washington 98011-9512

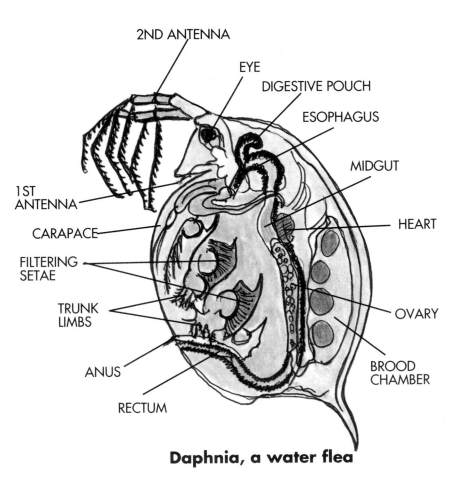

**Daphnia, a water flea**

2ND ANTENNA
EYE
DIGESTIVE POUCH
ESOPHAGUS
MIDGUT
1ST ANTENNA
CARAPACE
HEART
FILTERING SETAE
TRUNK LIMBS
OVARY
ANUS
BROOD CHAMBER
RECTUM

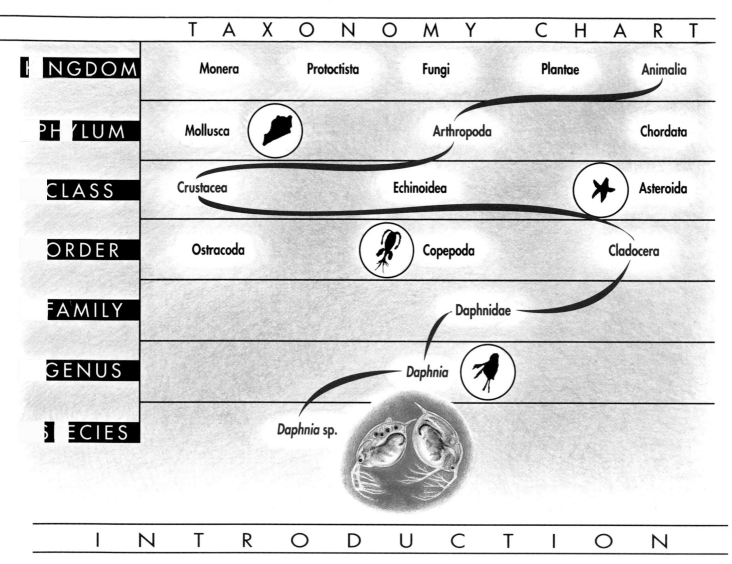

| KINGDOM | Monera | Protoctista | Fungi | Plantae | Animalia |
|---|---|---|---|---|---|
| PHYLUM | Mollusca | | Arthropoda | | Chordata |
| CLASS | Crustacea | Echinoidea | | | Asteroida |
| ORDER | Ostracoda | Copepoda | | | Cladocera |
| FAMILY | | | Daphnidae | | |
| GENUS | | *Daphnia* | | | |
| SPECIES | *Daphnia sp.* | | | | |

## I N T R O D U C T I O N

Do you remember the last time you felt lonely? The next time you think you're all alone, think again. Even if your room *looks* empty, you've got company. Millions of living critters are hidden in places you never thought to look: inside your intestines and your vacuum cleaner, for instance, and under your mattress, around your eyelashes, and even in your blood and the air you breathe. Just because you can't see them doesn't mean they're not there.

The micro monsters (microorganisms) in this book can be grouped together because they are all extremely difficult (or impossible) to see without the aid of a microscope. They're all living, of course! Well, all except the influenza virus on page 8. Scientists still disagree on whether a virus is a simple form of life or just a complex molecule, which is a stable group of atoms and electrons.

Some of these micro monsters are "monstrous" because they cause harm to other living things. Others only look like monsters when they are magnified fifty or a hundred times. Many of the photos in this book have been taken with the aid of a scanning electron microscope (SEM).

All scientists use one system to keep track of the millions of animal and plant species on Earth. That system is called taxonomy, and it starts with the five main (or broadest) groups of all living things, the kingdoms. (The micro monsters in this book represent all five scientific kingdoms.) Taxonomy then divides those into the next groups down—phylum, then class, order, family, genus, and, finally, species. Members of a species look similar, and they can reproduce with each other.

For an example of how taxonomy works, follow the highlighted lines above to see how the daphnia (*Daphnia* sp.) is classified. In this book, the taxonomic scientific name of each creature is listed next to the common name. In a few cases, only the scientific family or species name is used. Remember, cells do not have taxonomic names, but unicellular (single-celled) organisms do.

Turn to the glossarized index if you're looking for a specific micro monster, or for special information (where bacteria live, for instance), or for the definition of a word you don't understand.

## RED BLOOD CELL (Erythrocyte)

MARY SUNDSTROM

The cell is the basic unit of life. It is the simplest structure able to perform all the activities of life. Living things grow and develop, reproduce, excrete wastes, and take in energy (food, for instance) and change it into a different kind of energy (moving, for example). But that's not all. Organisms (another way of saying "living things") also respond to outside stimuli, and their lives evolve as a result of interaction with their environment.

Some organisms are single cells (unicellular). Others (humans, for instance) are a combination of many specialized cell types. Our muscles, bones, brain, and skin are made of cells. Cells are also floating in our blood.

There are three classes of cells in blood. Red blood cells carry oxygen to the brain and other organs and aid in the transport of carbon dioxide. White blood cells aid in defense against disease. And platelets are involved in coagulation, or blood clotting. The most numerous of these are red blood cells, or erythrocytes (ee-RITH-row-sights). Each red blood cell has a lifespan of four months. After that, cells are likely to become damaged as they squeeze through small capillaries. As blood passes through the liver or spleen, damaged red blood cells are withdrawn from circulation.

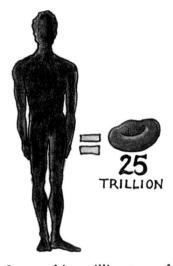

25 TRILLION

One cubic millimeter of human blood has about 5 million red cells. The average adult has *25 trillion* red cells! Red blood cells are manufactured in red bone marrow—at a rate of about 2 million per second.

The yellow blob resting on the red blood cell at right looks like a pat of butter, but it's really a platelet.

BETH EVANS

Photo, facing page © SPL/Custom Medical Stock Photo

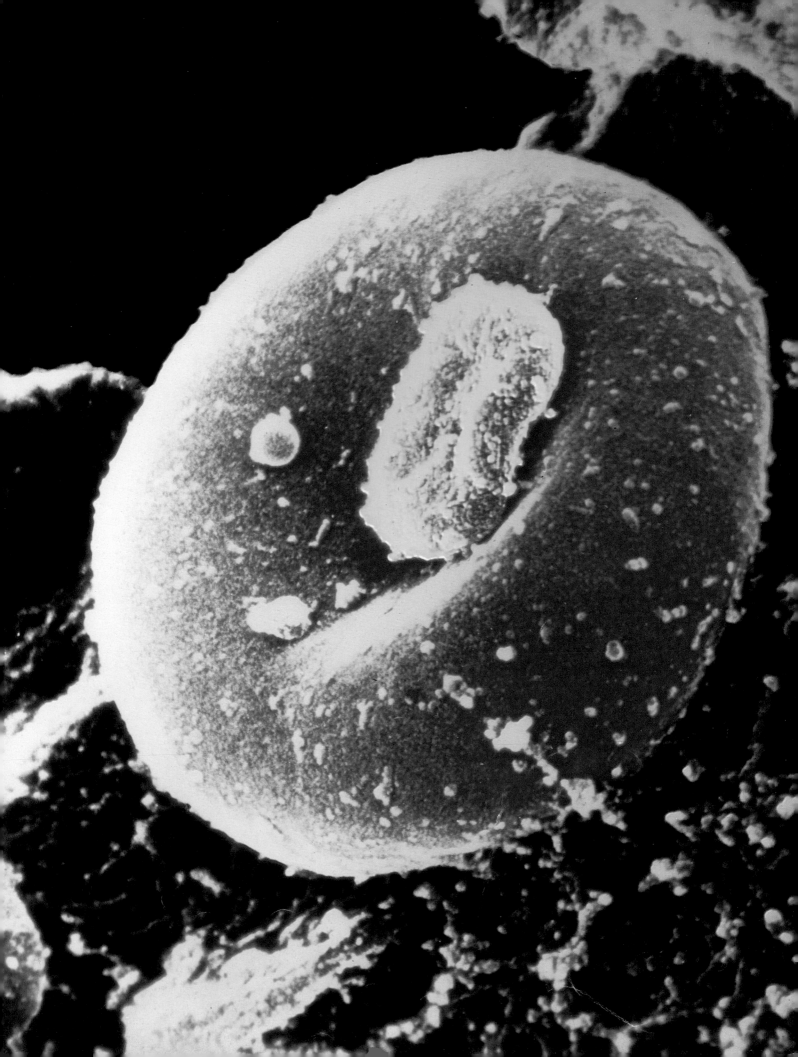

### BLOOD LYMPHOCYTE (Lymphocyte)

Every second of every day, foreign microorganisms such as bacteria and viruses are trying to invade your body. Don't panic, it's a normal part of life, and your body has ways to protect itself.

Skin and mucous membranes are your first line of defense against invaders. Your second line of defense comes from white blood cells—lymphocytes (LIM-foh-sights) and leukocytes (LEW-koh-sights)—which surround and destroy germs. They not only stop infection, they also clean up damaged tissue so healing can begin. There are five different types of white blood cells, and each does a slightly different job. Your third line of defense is the ability of some white blood cells to produce special chemicals known as antibodies. Different antibodies target different types of invaders, attach themselves to their outside surfaces, and stop or destroy them. Within a few days of the invasion, your blood is usually filled with antibodies. By the time the disease is over, the antibodies are gone, too.

Lymphocytes, also called T-cells and B-cells, are made in bone marrow but mature in your lymph glands and spleen. They are extremely important to your body's ability to defend itself. Helper T-cells recognize foreign invaders and alert the B-cells to make antibodies and memory cells that will help you in the future. Killer T-cells directly attack their target.

**Cells are made up of molecules. In turn, molecules are made up of atoms.**

**B-cells "remember" how to make antibodies that target a particular virus. If that virus—chicken pox, for example—enters your body again, you will be immune to it. That is, the cells will destroy the virus before it can make you ill again.**

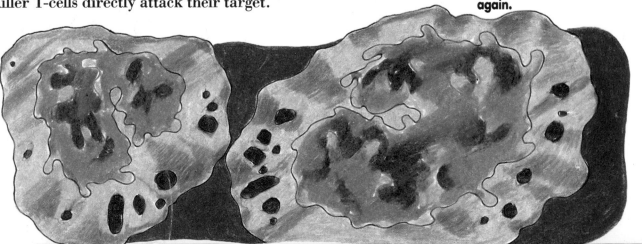

# MICRO MONSTERS

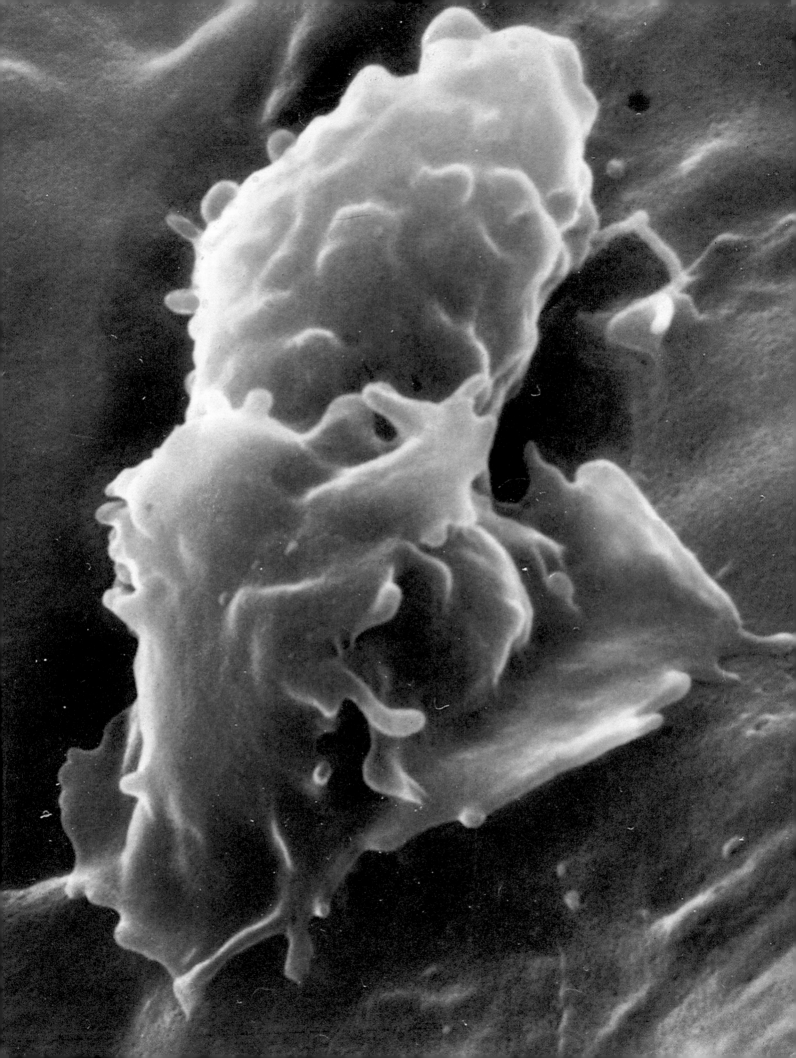

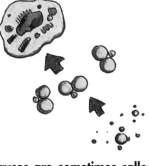

## INFLUENZA VIRUS

Are viruses alive? Are they the simplest life forms, or are they nature's most complex molecules? Scientists don't all agree on the answers to these questions. On the one hand, viruses are parasites, which means they live inside a "host" organism from which they take food or protection without giving anything back. And they can't reproduce independently, only inside living host cells. On the other hand, they do have a "genetic program," the biological information programmed in genes that makes each organism unique. Viruses can also evolve and change, another characteristic of living things.

But even if viruses are not living, they have a great impact on the biosphere. Many viruses cause disease, some in epidemic proportions. (An epidemic is a disease that spreads rapidly.) Both the common cold and the flu are caused by a virus.

Although the influenza virus pictured at right looks like a happy face, it can make humans very sick. Influenza viruses cause diseases such as Spanish, Asian, and Hong Kong flu. These flus occur all over the world, and they usually recur every ten to forty years because the virus changes its genetic program and human memory cells (remember the lymphocyte?) don't recognize it.

Viruses are sometimes called the "wheels of evolution" because they take pieces of one organism's genetic program and give it to another completely different organism. This helps to create biodiversity, the astounding variety of living things on our planet.

In 1984, researchers discovered that AIDS, which stands for Acquired Immune Deficiency Syndrome, is caused by a virus they named HIV. AIDS has become such a big epidemic many researchers now call it a pandemic. (*Pan* is Latin for *all*.) A pandemic has the potential to spread to every continent on the globe. HIV mutates (changes its genetic program) faster than any other virus ever studied by scientists.

Photo, facing page © B.S.I.P./Custom Medical Stock Photo

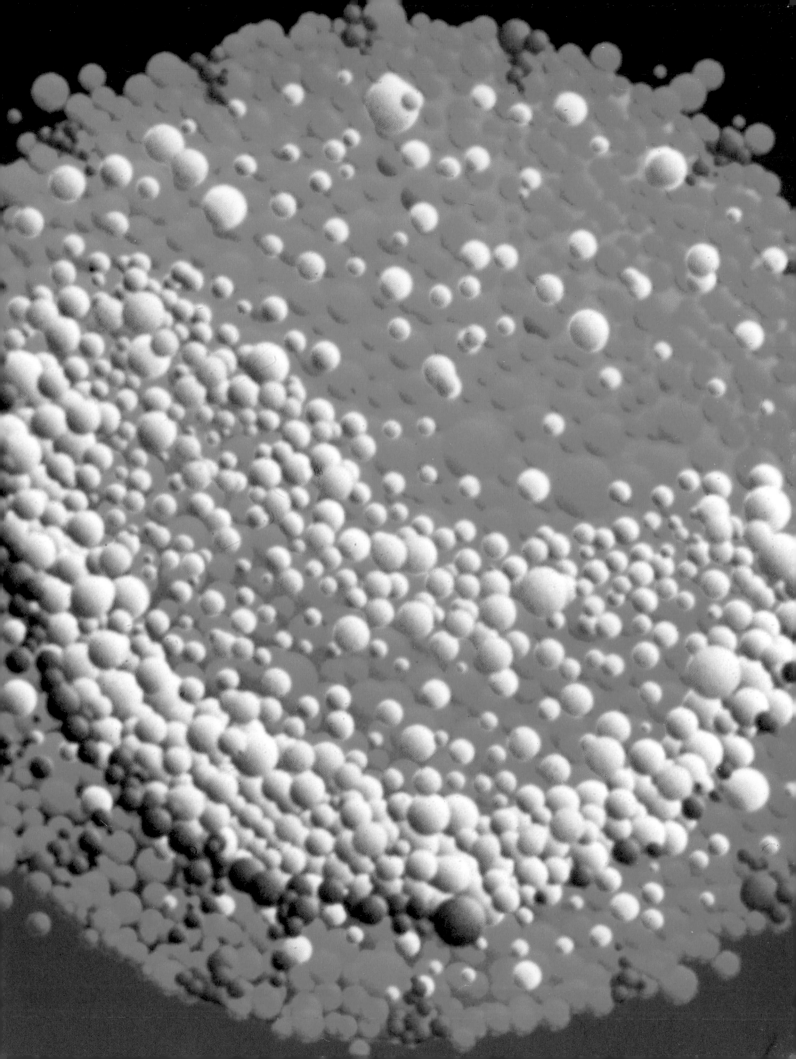

## PNEUMONIA (*Klebsiella pneumoniae*)

Bacteria live almost everywhere in the world: in Antarctic snows, vast deserts, near-boiling hot springs—and inside your intestines! There are 100 to 1,000 bacteria clinging to each square centimeter of your skin. Usually, these organisms are so tiny, 100,000 of them *together* can't be seen without a microscope. Some bacteria cause illness in humans and animals, but without them we and all other animals would disappear from the Earth. Bacteria are involved in food and oxygen production, and they are essential to cycling and recycling nutrients throughout the biosphere.

There are only about 2,700 known species of bacteria. That may sound like a lot, but compare it to 780,000 species of insects, 30,000 species of spiders, or 20,000 species of fishes. There may be fewer known types of bacteria than other creatures, but bacteria are the most abundant of all organisms. Most bacteria species have a recognizable shape. The three most common shapes are round, rod-shaped, and spiral-shaped. All bacteria cells have a simple cell structure with no nucleus, but they do contain a complete genetic program.

Bacteria are the only single-celled organisms that do not have a nucleus, the usually round, inner part of a cell that contains genetic codes and controls reproduction and growth.

The word "bacteria" refers to more than one of these organisms, "bacterium" to just one.

If you're infected by the bacterium at right, you'll probably catch pneumonia, a severe disease that causes inflammation of the lungs (painful swelling and irritation), weakness, and fatigue. Most pneumonia is treated with penicillin, an antibiotic.

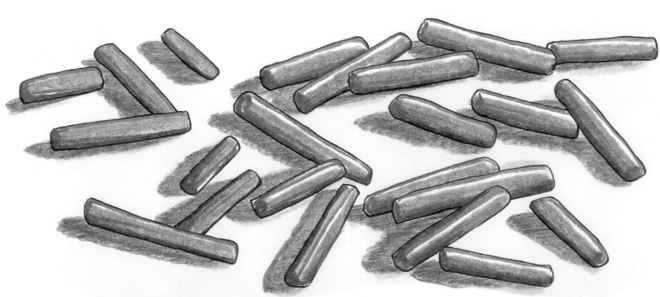

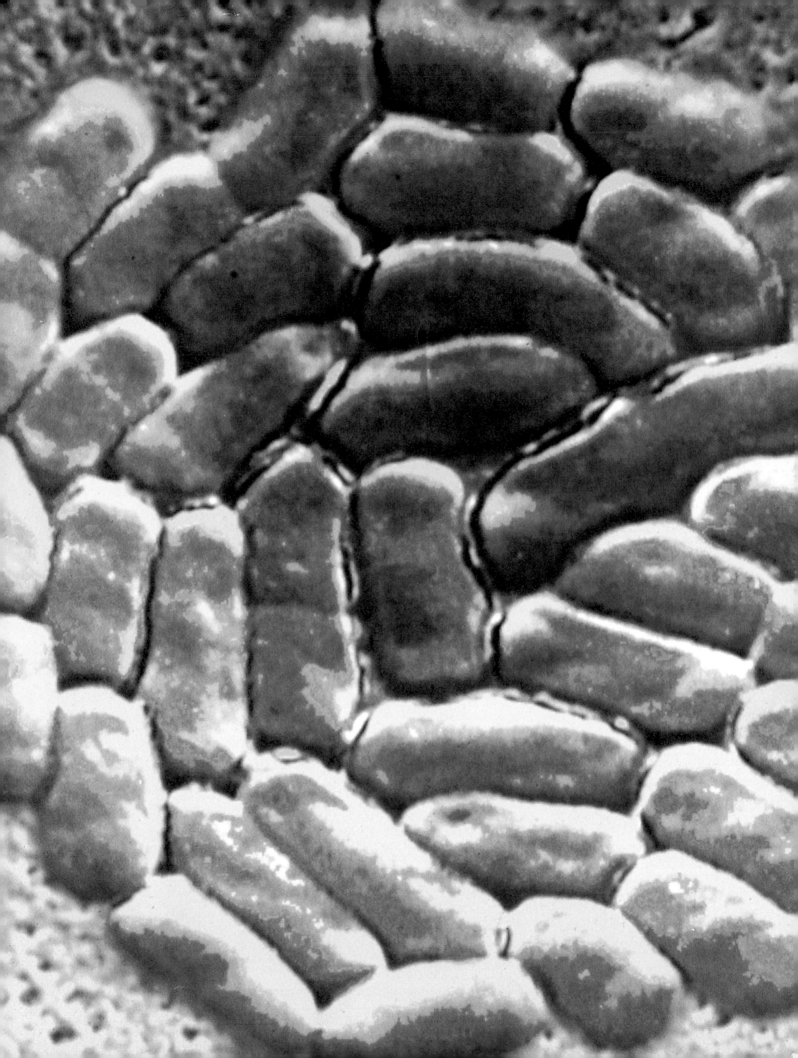

### BACTERIA (*Proteus mirabilis*)

*Proteus mirabilis* is a species of bacteria that plays an important role in microbial ecology because it helps decompose, or break down, organic matter so it can be reused as fertilizer by plants. The bacterium moves by waving its numerous flagella, threadlike extensions of its cell.

*Proteus mirabilis* lives in polluted waters and in manure, garden soil, and the feces of animals. It is also found in the intestines of some healthy humans, where it aids in the formation of urine.

But humans are mostly concerned with *Proteus* because it causes serious infections and can be resistant to some types of antibiotics. So, is this bacterium a "good guy" or a "bad guy"? When we judge another living organism as helpful or harmful, we are usually concerned with its direct impact on us. But every living thing is part of the web of life, and it's important to look at how each organism helps to maintain the biological and ecological balance on Earth.

*Proteus* was so-named by a scientist in the late 1800s because it reminded him of Proteus, the god in Greek mythology who was able to take different shapes.

**How many flagella can you count at right?**

Answer: Each *Proteus* has exactly 176 flagella.

**Bacteria are the simplest types of living cells. They are also one of the most successful life forms on Earth.**

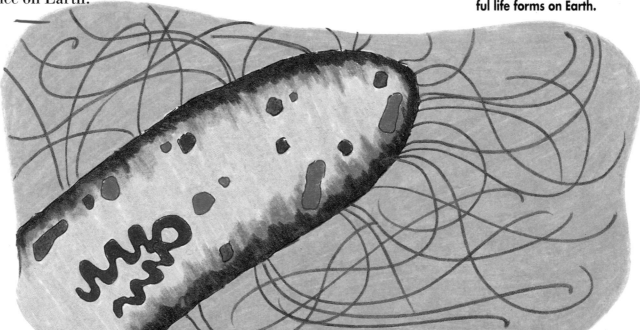

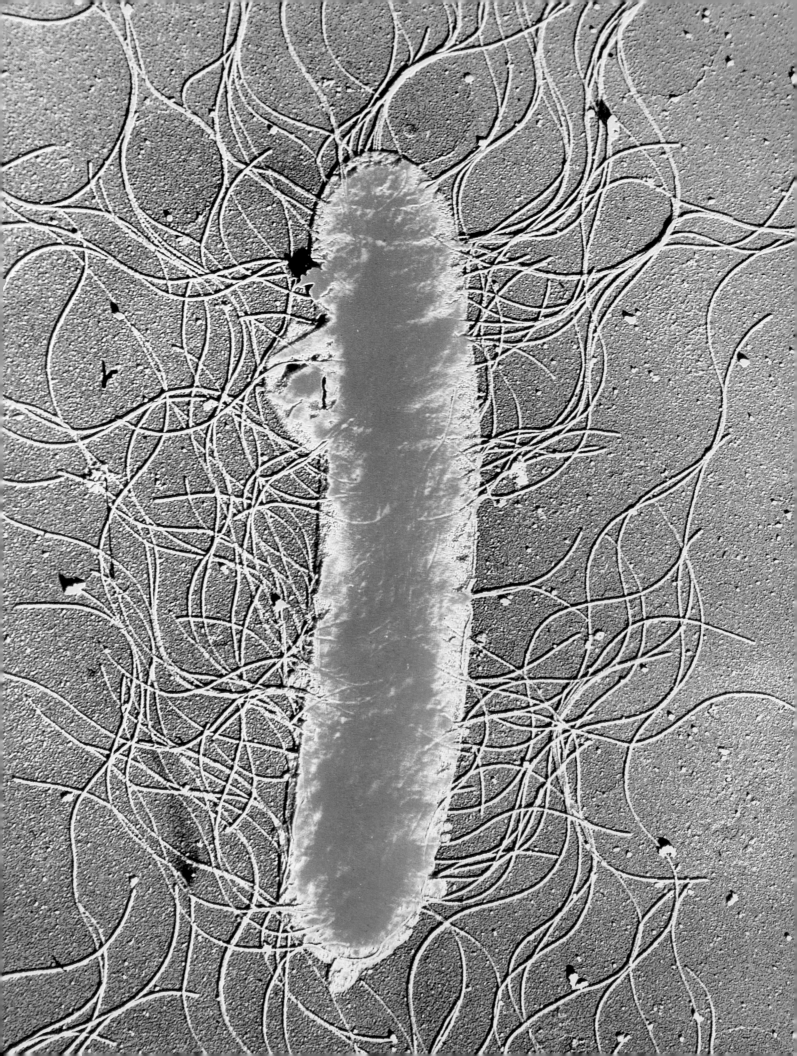

## YEAST COLONY (Phylum: Eucomycophyta)

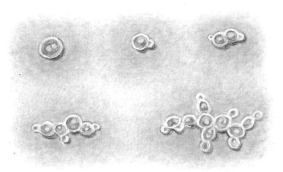

Members of the scientific kingdom Fungi include slime molds, molds, mildews, rusts, mushrooms, and yeasts. All fungi feed by dissolving and absorbing nutrients from dead plants and animals. They also reproduce by spores, and their main body is a mass of connected strands or threads. Together with bacteria, they are the principal decomposers that keep our soil renewed with nutrients.

Yeast is a single-celled sac fungus. Most sac fungi undergo sexual reproduction by forming spores within saclike cells. Sexual reproduction is the process of producing offspring from the cells of two different parents. But yeast is different. Most often, yeast reproduces asexually by budding. Bakers use yeast to make bread dough rise. Like all living things, as yeast grows it creates carbon dioxide gas as a waste product. The gas bubbles expand and cause the dough to expand, too. Yeast is also used to make beer and other alcoholic drinks.

Victims of a fungal disease known in the Middle Ages as St. Anthony's Fire suffered from nervous spasms, gangrene, hallucinations, and temporary insanity. The disease was caused by the consumption of grain contaminated by ergot fungi. An earlier epidemic, in 944 A.D., killed more than 40,000 people.

Plants and fungi moved from water to land at the same time. How do scientists know this? When they examine ancient terrestrial (earth-dwelling) plant fossils, they also find fungi. The oldest fossil fungi are about 450 to 500 million years old.

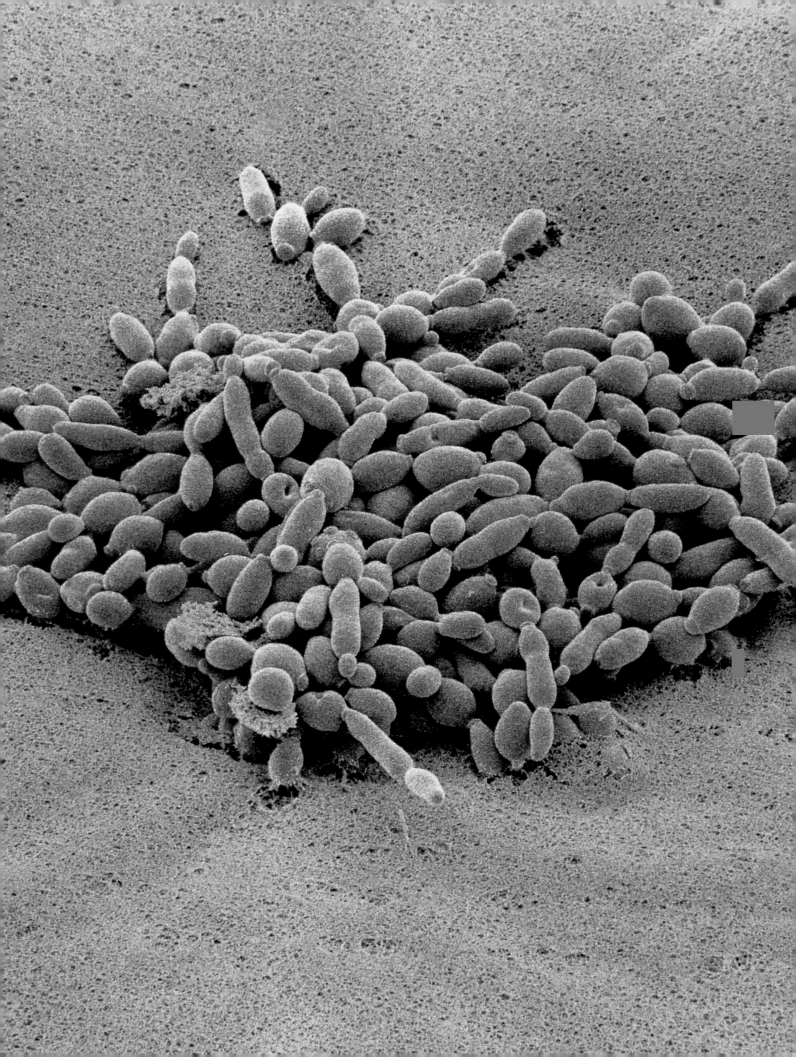

## PENICILLIUM (Phylum: Deuteromycota)

Penicillium—a blue-green mold—is a sac fungi like yeast. This mold grows on bread, wood, fabrics, leather, and other organic substances. Cheesemakers use penicillium to provide the peculiar flavor of Camenbert and Roquefort cheeses. Most important of all, this fungi produces the valuable antibiotic penicillin, which kills harmful bacteria without damaging healthy cells in our body. Its discovery and use changed the way the Western world treated diseases, and it greatly lowered the death rate worldwide. Today, most penicillin is synthetically produced in laboratories.

There are 100,000 known species of fungi, and scientists estimate there are 200,000 more to be discovered. All general types of fungi were in existence about 300 million years ago.

The plant called lichen (LIKE-en) is really a partnership. Lichen is made of a tiny plant called alga and a sac fungus. The alga supplies food for the fungus (because the fungus can't produce its own), and the fungus forms minute threads where the algal cells live. Because lichen is extremely sensitive to air pollution, it is used by the Environmental Protection Agency to determine air quality.

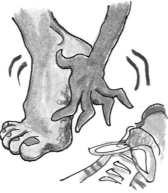

Many fungi cause problems for humans. Athlete's foot, ringworm, and lung infections may be caused by fungi. Plants are also at risk for fungi infections. Dutch elm disease, for instance, is a fungi that is devastating American elm trees.

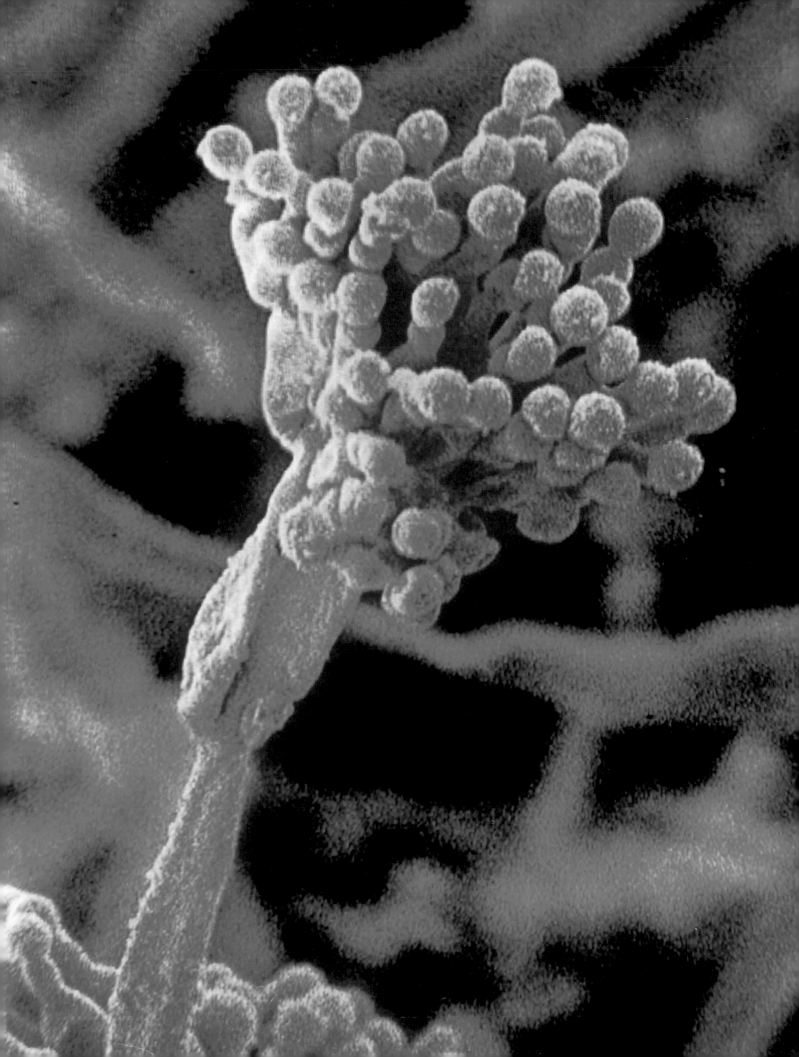

## DIATOM (Division (Phylum): Pediastrum)

Diatoms (DIE-uh-toms) are single-celled organisms found in oceans, lakes, rivers, and streams, where great numbers can turn the water green. In fact, one teaspoon of pond water may contain more than *a million* diatoms.

They also live on rocks and in soil—anywhere there's water. A diatom makes its own hard transparent shell, or frustule, by drawing the mineral silica from water. (Humans use silica to make glass.) The top of the frustule fits perfectly over the bottom of the frustule like a hat box.

There are almost 10,000 known species of diatoms. Although diatoms are tiny, they have big jobs. Diatoms (and some microscopic plants) create the oxygen that all organisms need in order to make energy. And aquatic animals feed on diatoms, which makes them an extremely important member of the food chain. The shells of dead diatoms pile up on the sea floor. Some deposits of these shells date from 10 to 70 million years ago and have become part of the continental land masses we humans live on.

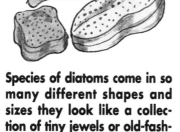

Species of diatoms come in so many different shapes and sizes they look like a collection of tiny jewels or old-fashioned buttons.

Gardeners use diatomaceous earth (earth made of crushed 10-million-year-old marine diatoms) to kill slugs. When the diatoms are crushed, their shards become sharp as glass!

Photo, facing page © R. Banfield/Custom Medical Stock Photo

# MICRO MONSTERS

## PROTOZOAN (*Epistylis* sp.)

Protozoans are animal-like unicellular organisms that are usually mobile. Some live in colonies (loose groups of cells), but each protozoan must take care of its own physiological needs. Protozoa are generally classified into four groups: flagellate protozoans (mostly parasitic), amoebid protozoans (such as amoebas), sporozoans (parasites), and ciliates (such as the predatory *Paramecium*, *Epistylis*, and *Stentor*, pictured below).

Most protozoans live in freshwater or marine environments, and they can exist wherever there is moisture. When their habitat dries up, protozoans form protective cysts, or envelopes. They can stay dormant until they contact water again and germinate (start to develop). *Epistylis* lives in groups called colonies. The colonies are often found living in the moss on the shell of the Western Painted Turtle.

Protozoans are so tiny that some develop in the salivary glands of insects. The insects then transmit them to new hosts through biting. For instance, one flagellate protozoan causes African Sleeping Sickness, a disease transmitted to humans by the tsetse fly.

Flagellate protozoans are named for their flagella, the long, threadlike extensions of their cells they use for locomotion. Ciliates are named for their cilia, the fringe of short, hairlike threads used to move food toward them or for locomotion.

Photo, facing page © Alex Rakosy/Custom Medical Stock Photo

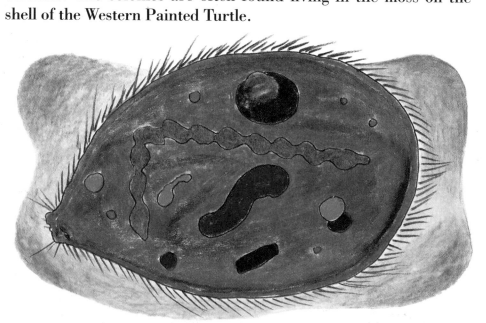

Although only a few dozen species of protozoans (out of thousands!) cause diseases in humans, as many as one-fourth of the world's human population may be afflicted by a protozoan infection.

## HUMAN HEAD LOUSE (*Pediculus humanus capitis*)

The human head louse belongs to a family of true (or sucking) lice that live and feed only on human primates. Besides the human head louse, humans also play host to the body louse (*Pediculus humanus corporis*). Other primates, such as chimpanzees and gorillas, host their own members of this true louse family.

Primate lice are part of a recent family in evolutionary terms. They are developing only as quickly as their hosts—we primates—allow them to. As we evolve and change, so do they.

True lice feed on blood that they draw from their host with their piercing and sucking mouthparts. They also need the vitamins they receive from the bacteria living inside their own minuscule bodies—which means there are parasites inside parasites. While the lice gain nutritional benefits, the bacteria live and breed inside their lice hosts. In fact, new generations of bacteria are transmitted to new generations of lice through the host eggs. In biology, this type of mutually beneficial living arrangement is known as symbiosis or mutualism.

While human head lice live in hair, human body lice survive on clothing or bedding and jewelry and only climb onto the skin to move around.

Fleas (relatives of lice) are incredible athletes. A member of one tropical species can average one jump per second for as long as 72 hours if it is excited by nearby fleas.

Photo, facing page, Animals Animals © Alastair MacEwen

### BEEF TAPEWORM (*Taenia saginata*)

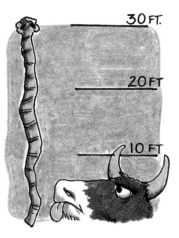

Tapeworms are parasites, and most have hooks and suckers on their head, the better to attach themselves to someone else. Although beef tapeworms have four egg-shaped suckers, they are called "weaponless tapeworms" because they sport no ring of hooks.

Young beef tapeworms reside inside the fat and muscle tissue of cattle, African zebus, and buffalo. How do they get there? By accident, when cattle and other large herbivores eat the tapeworm eggs in their food. Each egg envelope contains a hooked larva. When the cow's intestinal juices dissolve the envelope, the larva burrows freely through the intestines to reach the host's blood system. There it develops into a "bladder worm" that carries the head of a new tapeworm within it. But the tapeworm will never reach maturity unless it finds a new host—a person!

When people eat very rare meat or raw meat, they may also be eating a tapeworm. Once inside a human host, the ribbon of new reproductive organs located behind a tapeworm's head continues to grow. Sections of the ribbon separate into segments containing both male and female sex organs. Tapeworms are known as "egg millionaires" because by the time they are three months old, they release about a dozen ripe proglottids (egg envelopes) per day, each containing more than 100,000 eggs.

A single tapeworm can live for 30 to 35 years! It's pear-shaped head is about 1 to 2 millimeters in diameter and it may reach a length of 10 meters (over 30 feet).

Usually, there is only one tapeworm living inside each host. That's because many tapeworms would damage the host—and if the host dies, so does the tapeworm.

Photo, facing page © SPL/Custom Medical Stock Photo

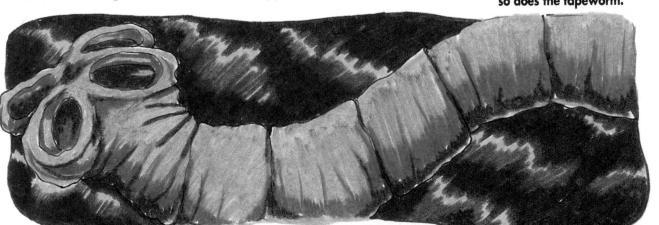

### INTESTINAL BLOOD FLUKE (*Schistosoma mansoni*)

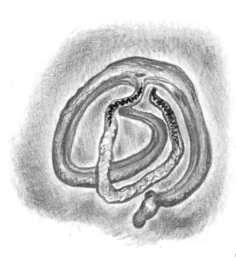

Blood flukes are parasites that live in the blood vessels of humans, their primary hosts. They cause the tropical illness schistosomiasis, an intestinal disease with flu-like symptoms. Different blood fluke species infect the bladder, the liver, and other organs in the human body. The intestinal blood fluke is found throughout Africa and in parts of South America and the West Indies.

Blood flukes always live as a pair; the threadlike female lies in the abdominal groove of the male. Fluke eggs make their way to the gut or bladder—causing much tissue damage—where they are eventually expelled. The larvae hatch in water and bore into their secondary host, a snail. After metamorphosis, they produce new larvae that swarm out of the snail and try to bore into a human host once again. People can only be infected in water, such as while swimming or working in irrigated fields. Once a larva has reached its human host, it is carried in the blood stream to the liver, where it matures.

Blood flukes are flatworms (so are tapeworms). Most flatworms are hermaphroditic, which means each one produces both eggs and sperm. Usually, they do not fertilize their own eggs.

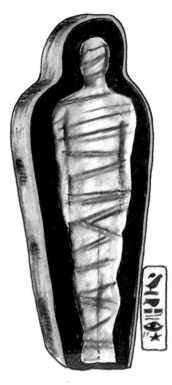

Health workers estimate that more than 100 million people are infected by blood flukes today. That's nothing new. Scientists know that ancient Egyptians suffered from the same parasite because they have discovered fluke eggs in mummies.

Photo, facing page © SPL/Custom Medical Stock Photo

# MICRO MONSTERS

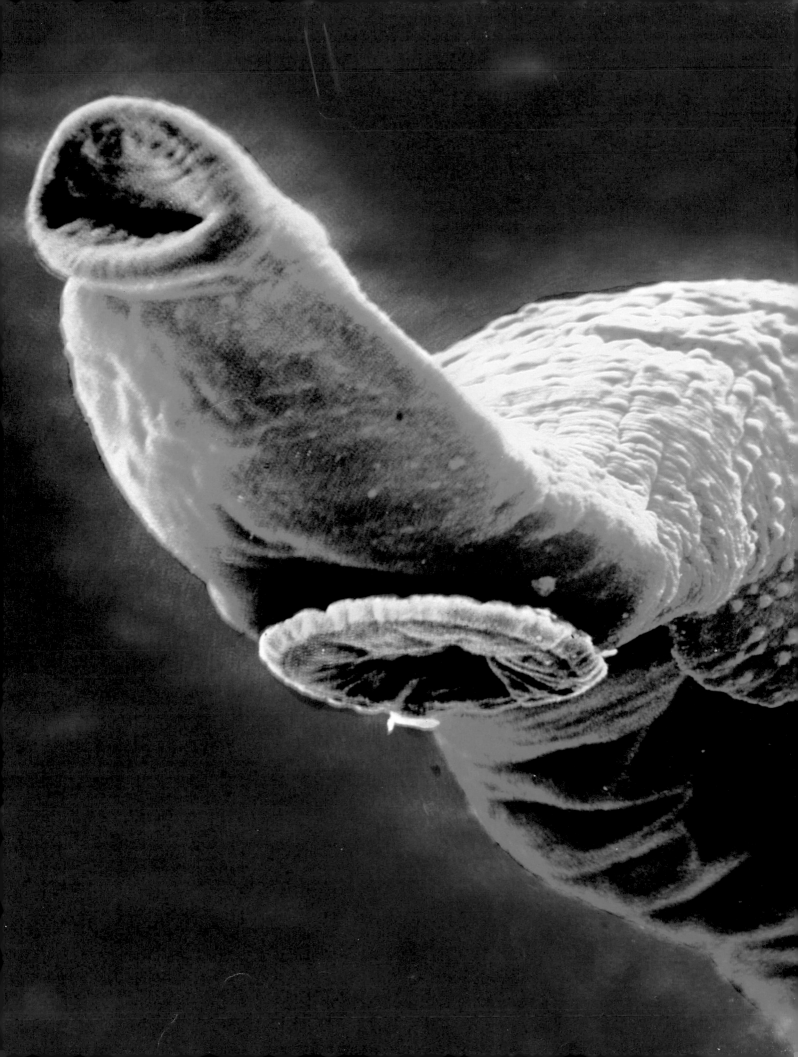

### DUST MITE (*Glycyphagus* sp.)

Have you ever imagined alien life on distant planets? What about inside your household vacuum cleaner? Mighty tiny dust mites thrive in damp homes, and they munch on furniture. Furniture?! Yep. They also scavenge stuffing, wallpaper paste, groceries, and whatever else is handy. This particular dust mite uses its front, saw-toothed claws to collect flakes while browsing through a pile of skin cells, soil particles, and cat fur. Of course it looks monstrous—in the photo at right it has been magnified more than a hundred times—but it's usually harmless to humans.

Mites also live in rugs, pillows, and beds. Beware, about 2 million bed mites are found in the average mattress, and they might make you sneeze. Some folks are allergic to dust mites. Vacuuming bedding every day can ease your sneezes, not to mention your asthma.

**Mites love to feed on skin cells. It sounds creepy, but remember that you shed millions of skin cells each day when you dress, scratch, brush, towel off, and toss and turn in bed.**

**Follicle mites are wormlike and they live head-down in the roots of some people's eyelashes. Eyelash mites use their eight clawed feet to get a grip. At night, when their host or hostess is sleeping, eyelash mites crawl out to find a mate or another resting place.**

Photo, facing page © SPL/Custom Medical Stock Photo

## RED SPIDER MITE (Family: Tetranychidae)

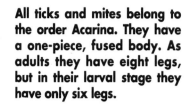

There are roughly 10,000 species of mites, including plant and animal parasites. Red spider mites are plant parasites, and they live on vegetables, fruit trees, and flowers, which they cover with their fine webs. They feed mostly by sucking out the juices of leaf cells, and they cause the leaves to turn brownish-yellow and fall off.

Some species of mites—marine mites, for instance—have adapted to life underwater. These able swimmers are usually brightly colored predators, and they feed on other water animals. What do you think cheese mites eat? If you guessed cheese, you're only partly right. They also eat ham, sausage, and bacon.

All ticks and mites belong to the order Acarina. They have a one-piece, fused body. As adults they have eight legs, but in their larval stage they have only six legs.

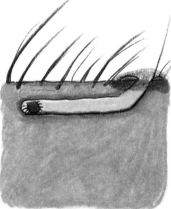

Watch out for the human itch mite! This critter bores into skin and makes tunnels parallel to the surface. It causes itching, scabs, and blisters, especially on soft skin, such as between the fingers and under the arms.

# MICRO MONSTERS

### TARDIGRADE (*Macrobiotus* sp.)

Although they are commonly called water bears, tardigrades are tiny—usually between 0.1 and 1.0 millimeter long—cylinder-shaped animals. (When have you ever seen a bear that was a millimeter long?) Tardigrades sport four pair of stumpy legs that end in large claws, the better to grip slippery surfaces. They need to get a grip because they usually live in ditches, lakes, coastal waters, and in moist, mossy clumps growing on rocks.

The nifty tardigrade can survive for months in a dehydrated capsule state known as a "barrel." When conditions are right, the tardigrade returns to normal size and shape. When it comes to feeding, tardigrades use their two needlelike stylets to puncture a moss cell wall and suck out the contents. But they are not total vegetarians; they have been seen capturing and feeding on the bodies of other water critters, such as nematodes.

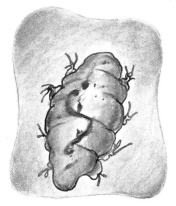

There are 300 to 400 known species of tardigrades. Because they are so tiny, tardigrades have no respiratory or circulatory organs.

The tardigrade at right has been magnified more than a hundred times. The long beanlike threads around it are algae.

Photo, facing page © Dr. Jeremy Burgess/SPL/Photo Researchers, Inc.

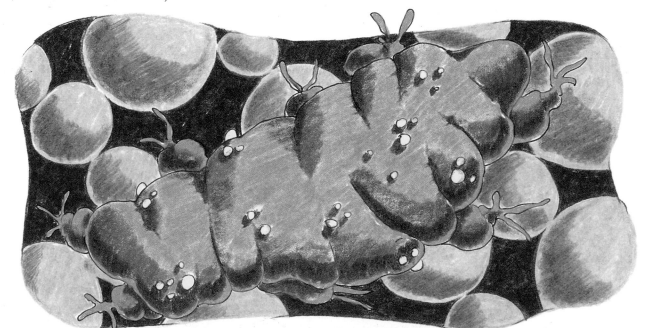

## WOODWORM BEETLE (*Anobium punctatum*)

Furniture made of wood is the woodworm beetle's habitat of choice. In the larval stage, this minute critter nibbles and gnaws a path through tables, chairs, and desks. When the adult emerges from its burrow, it leaves behind a tell-tale trail of dry, powdery sawdust.

The female woodworm beetle crawls and flies around the room searching for the perfect piece of furniture, a nice woody spot on which to deposit her eggs.

Although woodworm beetles and other types of boring beetles are not harmful to humans, they can be expensive. Some species do millions of dollars' worth of damage boring into furniture, lumber, wine crates, and even bottle corks. Other species are strictly outdoor types. They live in dead wood and, sometimes, live trees.

Some collectors pay lots of money for antique furniture with beetle "worm holes." Hoping to make a buck, furniture makers have been known to drill their own woodworm beetle holes.

What's so special about a beetle? For one thing, a beetle boasts a pair of tough front wings (called elytra) that protect the delicate wings folded underneath. A beetle's skeleton is sturdier than that of many insects. And its primitive mouthparts are able to chew solid food, allowing it to prey on other animals.

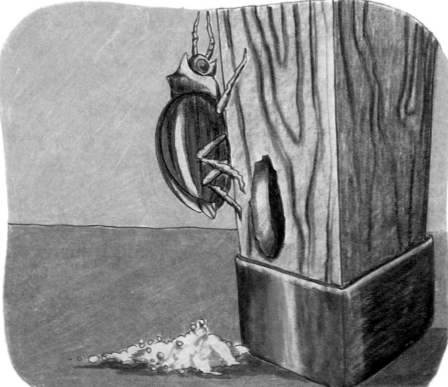

Photo, facing page © Dr. Tony Brain/Photo Researchers, Inc.

### DAPHNIA (*Daphnia pulex*)

The daphnia, a tiny freshwater flea, is a crustacean. Crustaceans range in size from microscopic freshwater and saltwater fleas to large lobsters. Typically, they have a segmented body covered with plates of tough skin, or carapace, and two pairs of antennae. Water fleas do have a carapace that encloses their body but not their head, which projects below their beak.

Daphnia is the most common water flea to be found on the surface of lakes and ponds. It uses its sturdy, fringed antennae as oars to pull itself up and down through the water. (It can't move forward and back.) As it cruises, it sweeps microscopic algae into its mouth. Water fleas brood their young in a rear chamber of their body and commonly reproduce by parthenogenesis, which means the eggs are not fertilized by the male and develop into females only. Eventually, changes in temperature or food supply spur the production of eggs that produce males.

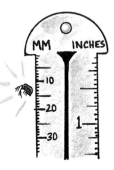

Adult daphnias may reach a total length of .2 to 3 millimeters (0.008 to 0.12 inches).

Daphnia and most other water fleas live in freshwater and filter tiny plant particles into their mouths. But a few marine water fleas are carnivores (meat-eaters). In turn, water fleas are a very important source of food for young fishes.

## COPEPOD (Order: Copepoda)

Copepods are small to microscopic crustaceans—marine and freshwater—and a source of food for fishes, mollusks, larger crustaceans, and other aquatic animals such as whales.

Copepod habitats vary from species to species. While many types are major members of marine plankton, others dwell on the ocean bottom, and some are parasites, infesting other aquatic animals.

While most copepods are extremely tiny (nearly microscopic), females may be visible to the naked eye when they carry two large egg masses. These animals are very effective when it comes to reproducing in great numbers.

Copepods are streamlined in shape, but they swim by jerky movements, using their trunk limbs as paddles and their second (not first) antennae as oars. The larger, first antennae pair serves a dual purpose: 1) it acts as a parachute against sinking, and 2) it may be used for rapid locomotion.

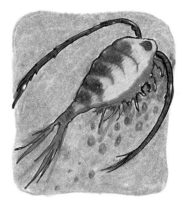

There are 4,000 species of copepods. They are a major food source for aquatic animals, in much the same way insects are a food source for land animals. Some copepods are filter feeders, which means they strain tiny particles through their mouthparts. Others use the bristles on their feet to collect particles of food.

Some species of copepods are known as cyclops because they have three simple eyes (called ocelli) that are often fused and so resemble one middle eye—just like the monster Cyclops!

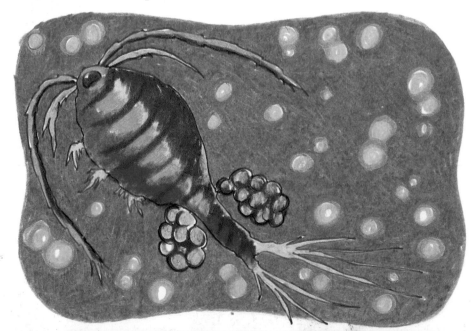

Photo, facing page © Alex Rakosy/Custom Medical Stock Photo

### MAIZE WEEVIL (*Sitophilus granarius*)

Weevils are tiny beetles who have hard shells and extremely long snouts. Their eyes, elbowed antennae, and mouthparts are set very far apart from each other. The family known as true weevils (numbering at least 50,000 species) is the largest family in the entire animal kingdom. True weevils are sometimes called snout beetles, elephant beetles, and billbugs because most sport an extremely long proboscis, or snout.

True weevils, such as the maize weevil, are herbivores (they feed only on plants), and they live all over the world. They have a reputation for being pests because they often bore into wood, leaves, seeds, and other plant tissue. The maize weevil belongs to a group known as grain and rice weevils. The larvae bore and drill into the stems, seeds, and roots of plants and trees. Grain weevils feed on everything from farm crops to breakfast cereal.

When disturbed, adult weevils pretend they are dead.

Biting jaws at the very tip of the weevil's snout (rostrum) are used to chomp down; the snout itself is a drilling tool. The snout-weevil's antennae "elbow" out from either side of the snout. At each antenna's tip, a "hairy" club allows the weevil to sense the plant seed or stem surface into which it is drilling.

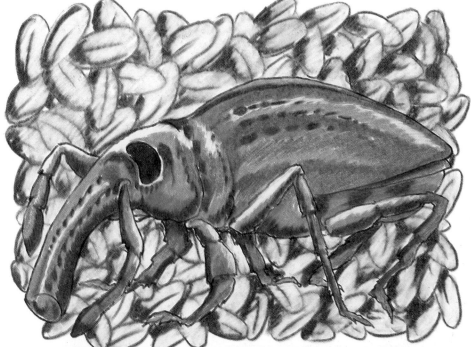

Photo, facing page © Dr. Tony Brain/SPL/Photo Researchers, Inc.

### SPRINGTAIL (Order: Collembola)

The springtail is an extremely primitive insect; its fossil record dates back 300 million years. Today, there are about 1,500 species (it's no wonder the one at right is unidentified), and they all belong to the scientific order Collembola.

Springtails live in varied habitats, but most species prefer moist places. They feed on rotting plant or animal matter, and perhaps on algae and diatoms.

Some springtail species have a nifty habit of using their tails to spring into the air. This particular springtail (in the photo) sports no springing appendage because it lives below ground. It is pictured wandering through peat moss.

All springtails are wingless, and their eyes are primitive ocelli made up of six to eight light-sensitive cells. Most species are only a few millimeters or less in length.

The springtail at right has been magnified about 40 times. Like many of the photos in this book, this picture was taken with a scanning electron microscope (SEM). The image is produced by aiming a beam of electrons at the object or creature. The photographer then studies the resulting electron reflections on a special TV. This provides a vivid three-dimensional picture of the specimen.

Springtails are found all over the world, including in Arctic and Antarctic regions. One extremely unusual species of springtail, the snow flea, gathers in great numbers on top of snow, even on glacier snow fields.

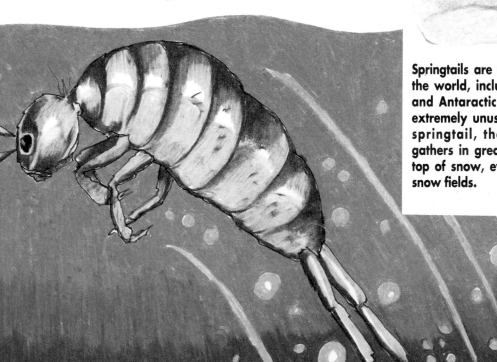

Photo, facing page © Dr. Jeremy Burgess/SPL/Photo Researchers, Inc.

## BEE LOUSE (*Braula coeca*)

The wingless bee louse is so tiny, it clings to the back of queen and drone honeybees and feeds directly from its host's mouth. As many as 180 bee lice can feed on a queen bee. While worker bees feed the queen, the louse sits on her head and sucks food right off her tongue. Like other parasites, the bee louse takes nourishment and shelter from its host without returning the favor.

Bee lice live in bee hives, where they deposit their eggs. After they hatch, bee louse larvae feed on the wax of the honeycomb that contains pollen. Scientists used to think there was only one species of bee louse, *Braula coeca*, which lives in Africa, Europe, and North and South America. Recently, however, they discovered a second species in Africa.

The wingless bee louse at right is resting on the back of a bee!

Many species of wingless flies die off because they can't escape their enemies or colonize new regions. However, one species of wingless fly is thriving on small, storm-swept islands in the Indian Ocean. It might not sound like a very nice place to live, but the violent winds destroy flying insects that would otherwise compete with the fly for food.

Photo, facing page © Dr. Brad Amos/SPL/Photo Researchers, Inc.

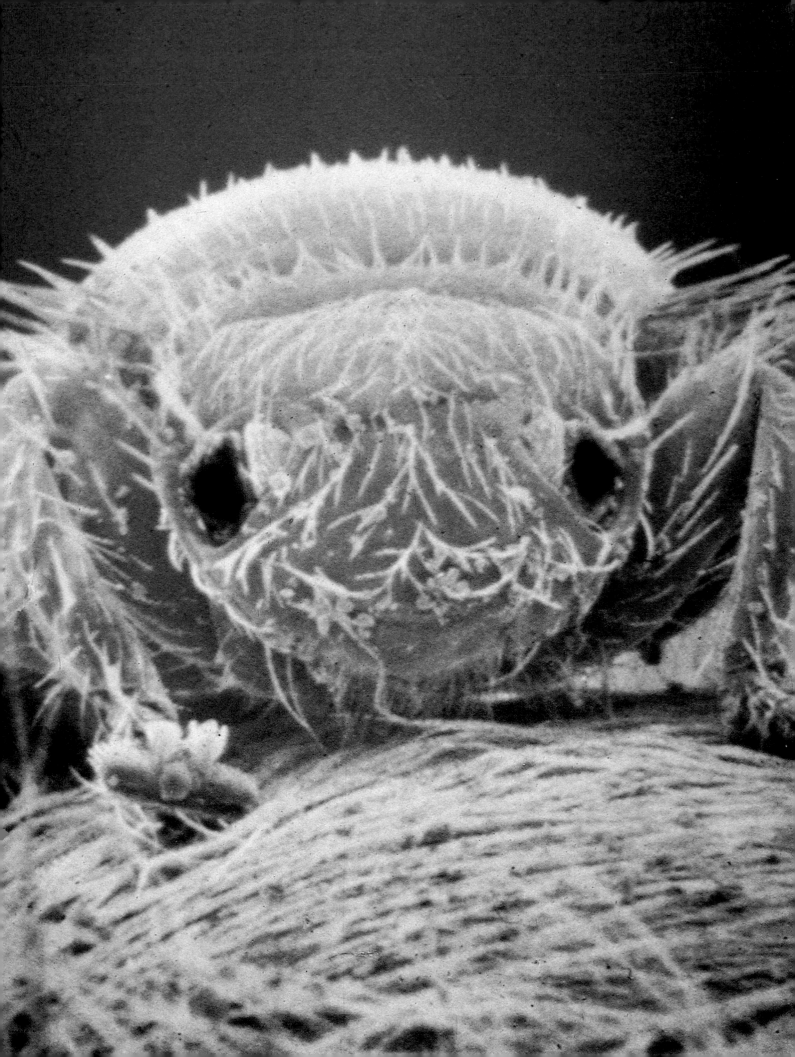

### SHEEP KED (*Melophagus ovinus*)

The sheep ked is wingless, and for a long time it was mistaken for a tick. Actually it's a parasitic fly. By any name, the ked makes life a pain for domestic sheep and sheep farmers because it sucks the blood of the animals, causing skin irritation and lowering wool production.

Sheep ked larvae are retained in the adult female's body until they are almost fully matured. They are fed by the juices of special glands in the female. They then attach to the sheep's wool until they reach maturity. When fully grown, this parasite may reach a length of 6 millimeters (about ¼-inch).

Other louse flies live in the feathers of birds or in the fur of elk and deer, where they suck their host's blood. Many species of louse flies lose their wings when they settle on a host, but the sheep ked is wingless all its life.

Bat flies are blind, wingless louse flies that live on bats. When the bats roost in close quarters, the louse flies travel from one host to another with the greatest of ease.

Photo, facing page © © Biophoto Associates/Photo Researchers, Inc.

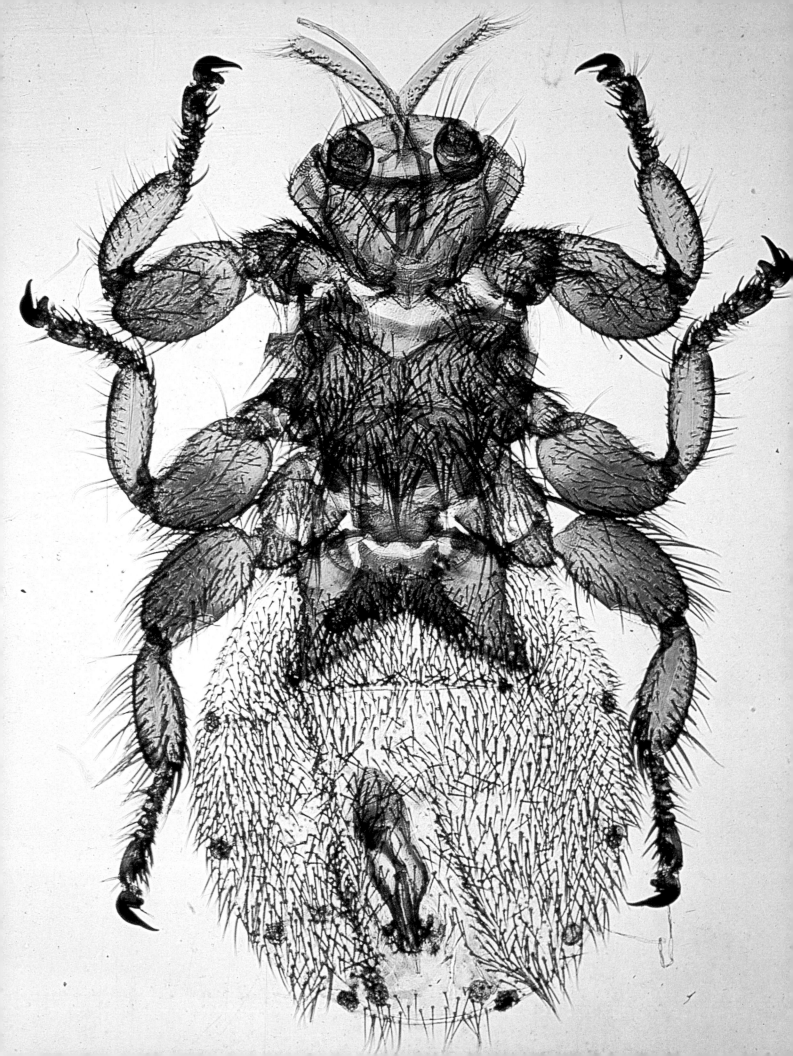

This glossarized index will help you find specific information on the cells and creatures in this book. It will also help you understand the meaning of some of the words used in the text.